Donated To The Library By

Mr. & Mrs. Donald Smith

CHRISTMAS 2003

©Highsmith® Inc. 1999

LIFEVIEWS

Published by Creative Education
123 South Broad Street, Mankato, Minnesota 56001
Creative Education is an imprint of The Creative Company

Art direction by Rita Marshall; Production design by The Design Lab

Photographs by Galyn C. Hammond, The Image Finders (Mark Gibson, Werner Lobert,
William Manning), JLM Visuals (Richard P. Jacobs, Breck P. Kent, Craig Kesselheim, John Minnich),
Robert McCaw, Tom Myers, James P. Rowan, Eugene G. Schulz, Tom Stack & Associates (Erwin &
Peggy Bauer, Tommy Dodson, Terry Donnelly, Jeff Foott, Robert Fried, Lynn Geri, Sharon Gerig,
Joe McDonald, Peter Mead, Milton Rand, Doug Sokell, Dave Watts, Jim Yokajty)

Library of Congress Cataloging-in-Publication Data

George, Michael.
Deserts / by Michael George.
p. cm. — (LifeViews)
ISBN 1-58341-251-4
1. Deserts—Juvenile literature. I. Title. II. Series.
GB612 .G46   2003
551.41'5—dc21   2002034787

First Edition

2 4 6 8 9 7 5 3 1

GARDENS OF SAND

DESERTS

MICHAEL GEORGE

THE WORD "DESERT"

makes many people think of shriveled cacti, sun-scorched sand dunes, and shimmering waves of heat. They assume that the desert is a lifeless, waterless wasteland, baked by the sun and battered by the wind. Yet despite its barren appearance, the desert is a fascinating place filled with unusual **beauty**. It is decorated with spectacular landscapes and is inhabited by an amazing variety of plants and animals.

Deserts are areas that receive, on average, less than 10 inches (25 cm) of **rain** per year. However, the amount of rainfall in a desert may vary greatly from month to month and from year to year.

Deserts are lands of heat, drought, and beauty.

In fact, deserts often go without a single drop of rain for 10 or 20 years. When it finally does rain, it pours. Ten inches (25 cm) of rain can fall from the skies within only a few hours.

Deserts cover about 20 percent of Earth's land surface (an area about the size of Africa). The largest desert, the **Sahara** in northern Africa, is almost as large as the continent of Europe. The Great Australian Desert is the second largest desert in the world. It covers about half of the continent of Australia. Other major deserts include the Arabian Desert and the Gobi Desert, both located in Asia. Smaller deserts extend down the western coasts of North and South America.

The arctic **tundra** also qualifies as a desert, based on annual rainfall. On average, this region receives less than 10 inches (25 cm) of precipitation each year, usually in the form of ice and snow. However, besides a lack of moisture, most deserts also have extremely high **temperatures**. Since the temperature rarely rises above freezing in the Arctic, this region is not a typical desert.

Most deserts are notoriously hot because of their lack of

All deserts lack rainfall, but not all deserts are hot. The arctic tundra (bottom)— a "desert" located in the northernmost lands of the world—may experience temperatures as low as -40 °F (-40 °C) during the winter.

rain and other forms of moisture. In humid regions, clouds and water vapor prevent much of the sun's energy from reaching the ground. But in dry, cloudless deserts, there is very little moisture to block the sun's **rays**. As a result, air temperatures commonly reach 110 °F (43 °C), and occasionally soar as high as 125 °F (52 °C)—and that is in the shade! The ground gets even hotter than the air; with little to shield it from the sun's rays, the desert floor can reach a temperature of 175 °F (79 °C).

Although the desert can be scorching during the day, it can be downright cold at night. After the sun sinks below the horizon, air temperatures can fall to a chilly 40 or 50 °F (4–10 °C). In the Sahara Desert, the temperature once fell from a midday high of 126 °F (52 °C) to a nighttime low of 26 °F (-3 °C)!

Deserts have low nighttime temperatures for the same reason that they have high daytime temperatures. In humid areas, moisture and clouds not only prevent the sun's energy from reaching the ground during the day, but also prevent

The saguaro cactus has a tremendous capacity to store water. Amazingly, this giant, which can reach a height of 15 to 50 feet (5–15 m), is supported by a tap root just three feet (.9 m) long.

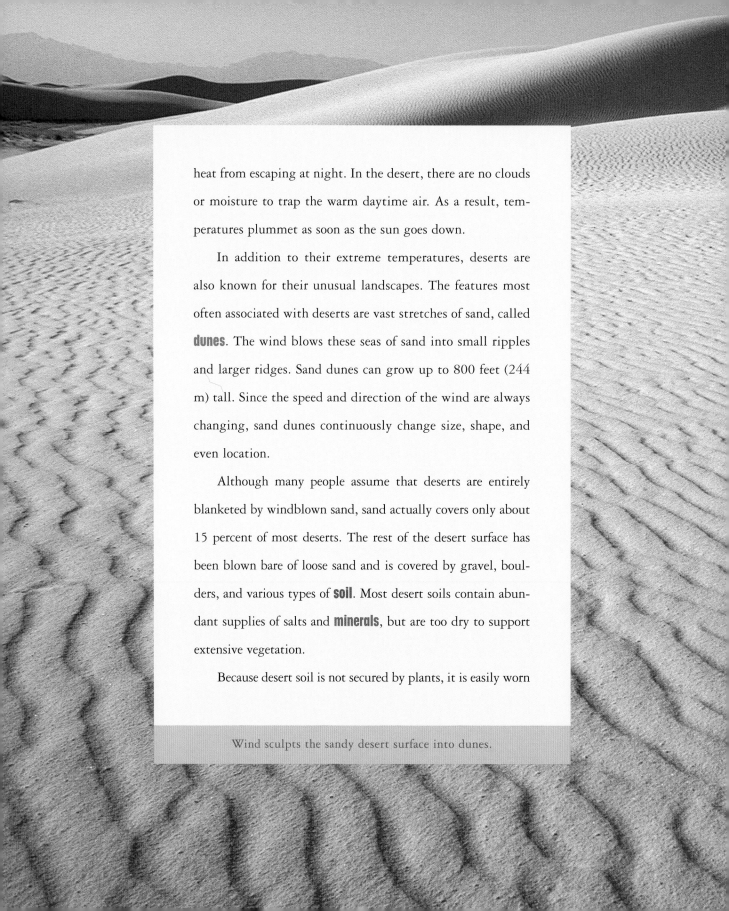

heat from escaping at night. In the desert, there are no clouds or moisture to trap the warm daytime air. As a result, temperatures plummet as soon as the sun goes down.

In addition to their extreme temperatures, deserts are also known for their unusual landscapes. The features most often associated with deserts are vast stretches of sand, called **dunes**. The wind blows these seas of sand into small ripples and larger ridges. Sand dunes can grow up to 800 feet (244 m) tall. Since the speed and direction of the wind are always changing, sand dunes continuously change size, shape, and even location.

Although many people assume that deserts are entirely blanketed by windblown sand, sand actually covers only about 15 percent of most deserts. The rest of the desert surface has been blown bare of loose sand and is covered by gravel, boulders, and various types of **soil**. Most desert soils contain abundant supplies of salts and **minerals**, but are too dry to support extensive vegetation.

Because desert soil is not secured by plants, it is easily worn

Wind sculpts the sandy desert surface into dunes.

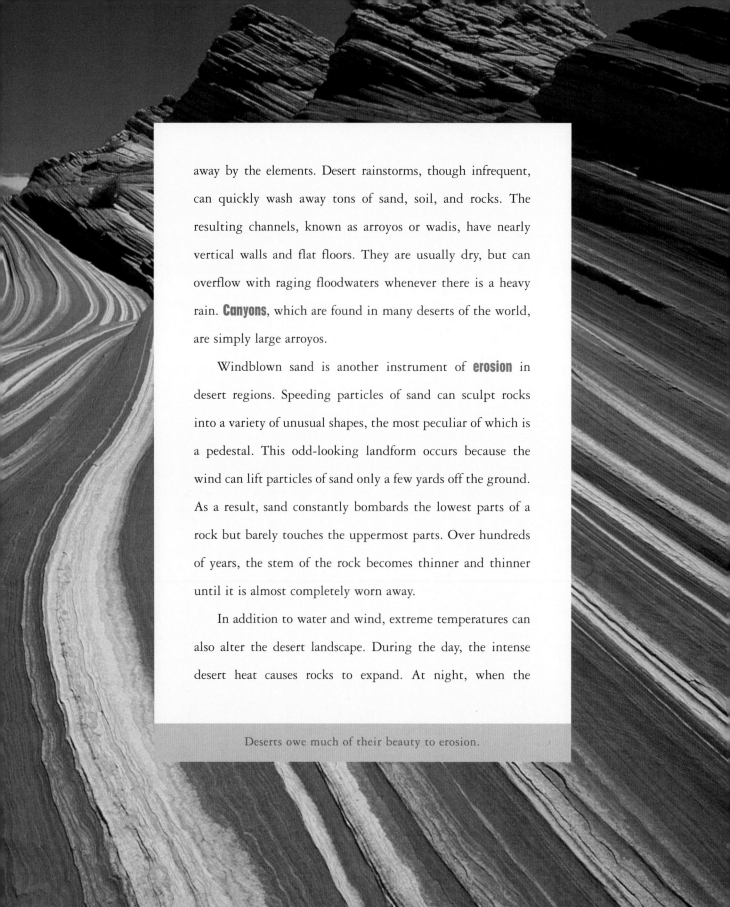

away by the elements. Desert rainstorms, though infrequent, can quickly wash away tons of sand, soil, and rocks. The resulting channels, known as arroyos or wadis, have nearly vertical walls and flat floors. They are usually dry, but can overflow with raging floodwaters whenever there is a heavy rain. **Canyons**, which are found in many deserts of the world, are simply large arroyos.

Windblown sand is another instrument of **erosion** in desert regions. Speeding particles of sand can sculpt rocks into a variety of unusual shapes, the most peculiar of which is a pedestal. This odd-looking landform occurs because the wind can lift particles of sand only a few yards off the ground. As a result, sand constantly bombards the lowest parts of a rock but barely touches the uppermost parts. Over hundreds of years, the stem of the rock becomes thinner and thinner until it is almost completely worn away.

In addition to water and wind, extreme temperatures can also alter the desert landscape. During the day, the intense desert heat causes rocks to expand. At night, when the

Deserts owe much of their beauty to erosion.

temperature drops, the rocks contract. Expanding and contracting, day after day and year after year, the rocks gradually weaken and fall apart. The pieces are eventually washed away by water or worn away by windblown sand.

The combination of water, wind, and temperature changes creates some of the desert's most spectacular landforms. Among these are buttes and mesas—solitary, steep-sided **plateaus** that rise high above the desert floor. Buttes and mesas consist of rock that is relatively hard and more resistant to erosion than the surrounding soil. Over hundreds of years, the surrounding land is weakened by changing temperatures and worn away by wind and water. Eventually, all that remains are the erosion-resistant buttes and mesas.

Decorated with sand dunes, arroyos, pedestals, and mesas, deserts are areas of unusual beauty. But perhaps the most magnificent desert landmark is the solitary **oasis**. An oasis is an area in the desert where there is a continuous supply of flowing water. Most oases are fed by underground springs. Since living organisms need water to survive, and

Only the hardest rock can withstand the erosive powers of desert rainstorms, winds, and extreme temperature changes. Piles of worn-away rock debris, called talus, litter many desert floors.

water is a scarce commodity in the desert, oases are always surrounded by an abundance of plant and animal life.

To many people, a desert oasis appears to be an island of life in an otherwise lifeless sea of dust. Yet despite its barren appearance, the desert is inhabited by a remarkable **variety** of plants and animals. In order to survive in the dry, hot desert, these organisms have developed some unusual characteristics and behaviors.

Plants, like all living things, cannot survive without a regular supply of water. In order to collect enough life-sustaining water, many desert plants have **roots** that extend far from their stems. These roots absorb every drop of water from the seemingly dry desert soil. They are so efficient that other plants cannot grow nearby. As a result, vegetation in desert regions is usually sparse.

Some types of desert plants do not bother trying to wring water from the dry soil. Instead, they tap pools of water that

Despite the harsh growing conditions, an abundance of plant life thrives in the desert—from the tall saguaro cacti to the flattened prickly pear, from scraggly brittlebrush to vibrantly colored poppies.

lie hidden beneath the ground. For example, the mesquite tree has roots that plunge 40 feet (12 m) beneath the desert floor. Still other types of desert plants store water in their leaves, roots, or stems. The barrel cactus, for instance, swells with water after it rains and slowly shrivels during times of **drought**.

Perhaps the most original method of gathering water is that of the Welwitschia, found in the Sahara Desert. This unusual plant has long, gnarled leaves that collect morning **dew**. The dew drips off the leaves, soaks into the ground, and is absorbed by the Welwitschia's roots.

Besides having resourceful methods of obtaining water, desert plants also have ways to protect the valuable water that they collect. Since water **evaporates** quickly from leaves, many desert plants have tiny leaves. Other desert plants shed their leaves during dry periods. Plants also protect their valuable supplies of water with waterproof skins that limit evaporation, and spines that deter thirsty animals.

While most desert plants have ways to survive

The ocotillo (top) grows tiny leaves or no leaves at all to prevent precious water from evaporating. Africa's Welwitschia (bottom), on the other hand, grows strap-shaped leaves up to 20 feet (6 m) long to collect moisture.

extended periods of drought, some do not even try. These plants may lie for years as **dormant** seeds buried in the desert soil. They spring to life only after a heavy rainfall. The individual plants live only a few short weeks before they shrivel beneath the dazzling desert sun. But before they die, the plants scatter seeds that will spring to life during the next rainy season.

Animals, like plants, also have resourceful techniques for surviving in the desert. Many desert animals obtain moisture from morning dew or from the foods they eat. Other animals have more inventive methods for quenching their thirsts. The best-known desert animal, the **camel**, actually stores water for later use. A camel can drink 30 gallons (114 l) of water—nearly the amount needed to fill a bathtub—at one time. After drinking its fill, a camel can survive for a week or more without another drink of water.

Perhaps the most fascinating method of obtaining water is that of the sand roach, found throughout the

Equipped with special adaptations that allow them to tolerate extreme temperature changes and drought, a wide variety of insects, birds, mammals, and reptiles call the desert environment home.

deserts of the southwestern United States. This remarkable insect actually absorbs water from the seemingly dry desert air. Its unusual method of "drinking" is so efficient that a sand roach can live its entire life without a sip of water.

In order to survive in the desert, animals must overcome hardships besides the lack of water. The desert's extreme temperatures are another **threat** to life. Few creatures can survive temperatures that are consistently higher than 100 °F (38 °C). Therefore, animals try to avoid the desert floor during the day, when the temperature soars.

One way to escape the extreme heat on the desert surface is to **burrow** beneath the ground. The temperature drops abruptly only a few inches below the desert surface. The kangaroo rat is one of the many desert animals that spend their days underground; like most burrowing animals, it comes above ground only after sunset. These animals feed and drink at night, when temperatures are cooler. As a result, the desert seems almost lifeless during the day, but comes alive with foraging spiders, insects, and rodents at night.

Blistering daytime temperatures force many desert creatures below ground. Animals such as lizards, rodents, scorpions, and beetles burrow into the sand to stay cool until the sun sets.

Other animals escape the desert's midday heat by elevating themselves. Some types of **snakes**, for instance, climb into small shrubs during the day. Suspended just a few feet above the desert sand, the snakes stay significantly cooler and have a much better chance of survival. The camel also takes advantage of the relatively cool temperatures above the desert floor. Growing up to seven feet (2.1 m) tall, camels stand at a height where the temperature can be 50 degrees cooler than on the ground. Birds have the most effective method for escaping the hot desert surface. Hawks, eagles, and **vultures** soar high above the ground, where temperatures can be a comfortable 60 °F (16 °C) on even the hottest days.

A desert is a region of extreme drought, torrential floods, scorching heat, and bone-chilling cold. Yet despite these uninviting conditions, a desert is not a barren wasteland. Instead, it is a region decorated by **exotic** landscapes and inhabited by a variety of living things. A desert has a strange beauty that is found nowhere else on Earth.

Various textures, shapes, and colors define the desert landscape.

BOTTLE THERMOMETER

To measure temperatures in a desert, thermometers must be able to withstand extreme heat during the day and near-freezing conditions at night. This bottle thermometer has a very limited measurement range and would be ill-suited for taking readings in a desert, but the principles behind it are the same as those of any mercury or alcohol (liquid-column) thermometer. Liquid-column thermometers are often used in research because of their low cost and precision.

You Will Need

- Tap water
- Red food coloring
- A glass soda bottle or similar small-mouthed bottle
- A clear plastic drinking straw
- Modeling clay
- A permanent marker
- A pan
- A glass thermometer (to measure air and water temperature)

Building the Thermometer

1. Fill the bottle with warm tap water and add a few drops of food coloring.
2. Shape a small piece of clay around the straw, about two inches (5 cm) from one end.
3. Insert the straw into the bottle and mold the clay so that it seals the top of the bottle and holds the straw in place. Make sure the straw does not touch the bottom of the bottle.
4. Water will rise up the straw. Let the bottle stand for about an hour, until the water reaches room temperature and the level remains steady.
5. Draw a line on the straw to mark the water level. Then, check the thermometer and write the room temperature next to the line on the straw.

6. Fill the pan with hot tap water and set the bottle in it.

7. Wait until the water level stops rising and mark the new level. Check the temperature of the water in the pan with the thermometer. Write the temperature next to the new line.

8. Mark equally spaced lines between the high temperature and the low temperature, and label them accordingly. If, for example, your low temperature is 70 °F and your high temperature is 90 °F, make marks for 75, 80, and 85. If you use the Celcius scale and your low temperature is 20 °C and your high is 35 °C, make marks for 25 and 30.

Observation

Like mercury and alcohol thermometers, your bottle thermometer works on the principles of the expansion and contraction of liquids. When heated, water molecules move very rapidly and take up more space, or expand. When cooled, the molecules slow down and take up less space, or contract. This expansion and contraction causes the water to move up and down the straw.

COLOR AND HEAT

In a land where daytime temperatures regularly reach more than 100 °F (38 °C), the key to survival is staying as cool as possible. Resting in the shade, burrowing underground, and drinking water all help keep desert animals from overheating. Even being a certain color helps. Test this for yourself with two thermometers and two cloth squares of the same size and fabric, one white and one black.

First, lay both thermometers on the ground in the sun next to each other. After about 30 minutes, record the temperatures. They should be the same. Next, cover one thermometer with the white square and the other thermometer with the black square. Leave them in the sun for another 30 minutes and record the temperatures. Which color absorbed more of the sun's heat rays?

Sand-colored or white fur helps many desert animals such as the fennec fox and the jerboa beat the heat because of the fact that light colors reflect heat, while dark colors absorb it. For thousands of years, Bedouins, nomadic desert peoples of Asia and North Africa, have made good use of this knowledge, covering themselves in loose, white garments and turbans to ward off heat.

LEARN MORE ABOUT DESERTS

Arizona-Sonora Desert Museum
2021 North Kinney Road
Tucson, AZ 85743
http://www.desertmuseum.org

Blue Planet Biomes
(Online resource for information on
  Earth's major life zones)
http://www.blueplanetbiomes.org

DesertUSA.com
(Internet-based magazine devoted to
  North American deserts)
http://desertusa.com

The Living Desert Zoo & Gardens
47-900 Portola Avenue
Palm Desert, CA 92260
http://www.livingdesert.org

Mojave National Preserve
222 East Main Street, Suite 202
Barstow, CA 92311
http://www.nps.gov/moja

National Wildlife Federation
11100 Wildlife Center Drive
Reston, VA 20190
http://www.nwf.org/wildalive/
  tortoise/index.html

The Wild Camel Protection Foundation
School Farm
Benenden, Kent TN17 4EU
United Kingdom
http://www.wildcamels.com

INDEX

Some deserts receive just a few inches of rain each year.